A SHOW OF HANDS
say it in sign language
by
Mary Beth Sullivan
&
Linda Bourke

with Susan Regan
illustrations by Linda Bourke

HarperTrophy
A Division of HarperCollinsPublishers

A Show of Hands

Text copyright © 1980 by Educational Projects, Inc.
Illustrations copyright © 1980 by Linda Bourke
Originally published by Addison-Wesley.
Published in hardcover by J.B. Lippincott, New York.
For information address HarperCollins Children's Books,
a division of HarperCollins Publishers, 10 East 53rd Street,
New York, NY 10022.
First Harper Trophy edition, 1985.

Library of Congress Cataloging-in-Publication Data
Sullivan, Mary Beth
  A show of hands

  [1. Sign language—Juvenile literature.] I. Bourke,
Linda, joint author. II. Title.
HV2474.S94   419   84-48782
ISBN 0-06-446007-X (pbk.)

For Mom & Dad (L. B.)
and
For Al, with love. (M. B.)

We were fortunate to receive valuable support
for A SHOW OF HANDS as it grew. We offer our
appreciation here:
    To Alan Brightman and Joseph Blatt for their
standards, their suggestions and their friendship; to
Susan Regan for the hours of informative discussions
and candid recommendations; to Nancy Becker, Laurel
Chiten, Kim Schive and Carole Osterer for their
considered, substantive feedback; to Ann Dilworth,
Mary K. Harmon and the Children's Book staff at
Addison-Wesley for the impetus, supportive pressure
and endless optimism; to the Workshop on Children's
Awareness and Educational Projects, Inc. for their
enthusiasm towards us as individuals and for their
continued encouragement of efforts to increase the
world's awareness of disabilities.

Finally, with affection, we thank Gordon for the
inspiration.

WHAT'S INSIDE

LET'S BEGIN

Seven out of every 100 people in this country are deaf or hearing impaired. Many of these 14 million people communicate by reading lips and speaking. Many others use sign language—a language made up of particular hand shapes and movements.

A SHOW OF HANDS is about sign language. In it you will see how to "talk" with your hands and "hear" with your eyes.

Most people learn sign language because they are deaf or because they know someone who is, but A SHOW OF HANDS is for everybody. In fact, today, thousands of people are signing because it's expressive, because it's beautiful and because it's a lot of fun! So roll up your sleeves and get ready to let A SHOW OF HANDS show your hands a thing or two!

Who, Me?

YES, YOU!
The fact is, hands have been sending important messages for a long time.

Public figures, Native Americans and characters from children's literature are among the most noted for using hands to communicate or to help make a point.

Perhaps the most popular signs are those used by people
in sports. The umpire surely signaled gloom through
Mudville that fateful day Mighty Casey struck out.

We all use hands to communicate in many ways. Waving, pointing, shaking hands and touching are only a few short cuts for speaking. Your hands probably have quite a bit to say:

15

Love at First Sign

19

Are you a southpaw signer? You'll notice that all the signs in the book are made by "righties," so if you are a "lefty," simply switch them around to suit yourself.

PICTURE THIS

The language of signs is much more than a collection of random gestures. Each sign has a particular hand shape and a particular meaning. Some signs are easy to remember because they make a clear picture of the idea they represent. Banana is an a "peel"ing sign for this reason.

"PEEL" A BANANA

BANANA

CAMERA

TREE

SHAKE THE "LEAVES"

SPROUT YOUR HAND

GROW

22

ICE CREAM

MILK

BABY

23

TICKLE

KISS YOUR CHEEK

TICKLE YOURSELF

KISS

HOUSE

MAKE A ROOF AND WALLS

SPIDER

24

TELEPHONE

BUTTERFLY

MOTORCYCLE

BOOK

Flying High

BODY TALK

What your face and body say while you're signing is just as important as what your hands say. No one needs an interpreter to know this sign means "angry."

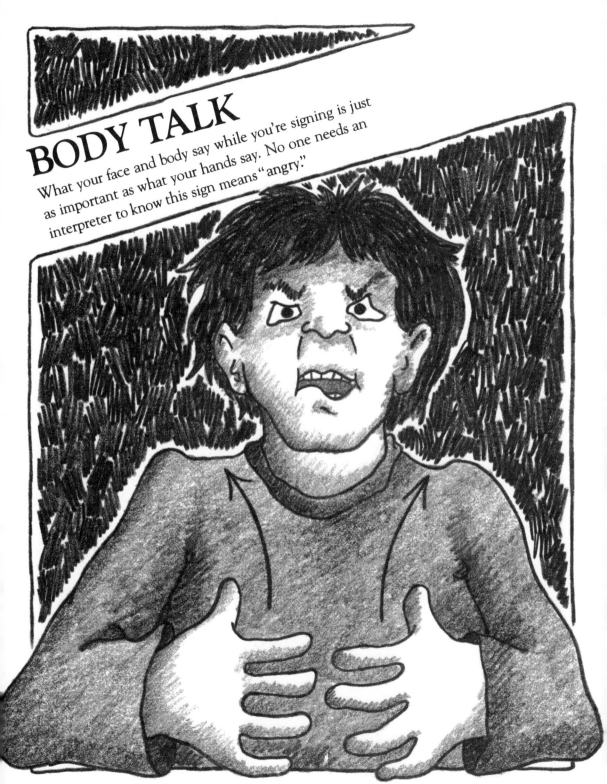

The exact meaning of a sign changes when your body language changes. Whether you have a "slight stomachache" or a "whale of a bellyache," you can use the same hand sign, but you must use different body and facial expressions:

It isn't always necessary to use a hand motion for "not" or "don't" because your face can say so for you. In fact, opposite facial expressions give opposite meanings to a sign.

Here's a puzzling problem: There's just one piece missing, but there are two left and *both* of them fit! Which is correct?

By themselves, hand movements only tell part of the message. . .

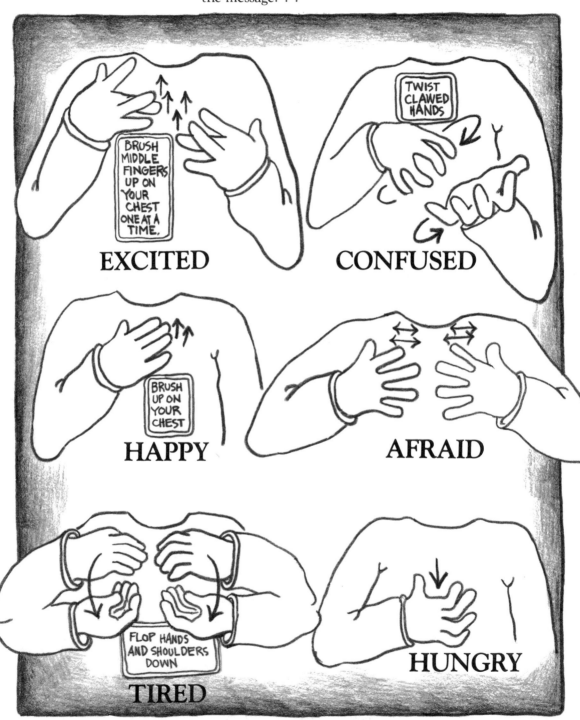

EXCITED

BRUSH MIDDLE FINGERS UP ON YOUR CHEST ONE AT A TIME.

CONFUSED

TWIST CLAWED HANDS

HAPPY

BRUSH UP ON YOUR CHEST

AFRAID

TIRED

FLOP HANDS AND SHOULDERS DOWN

HUNGRY

. . . but add a facial expression and you will understand
the whole idea.

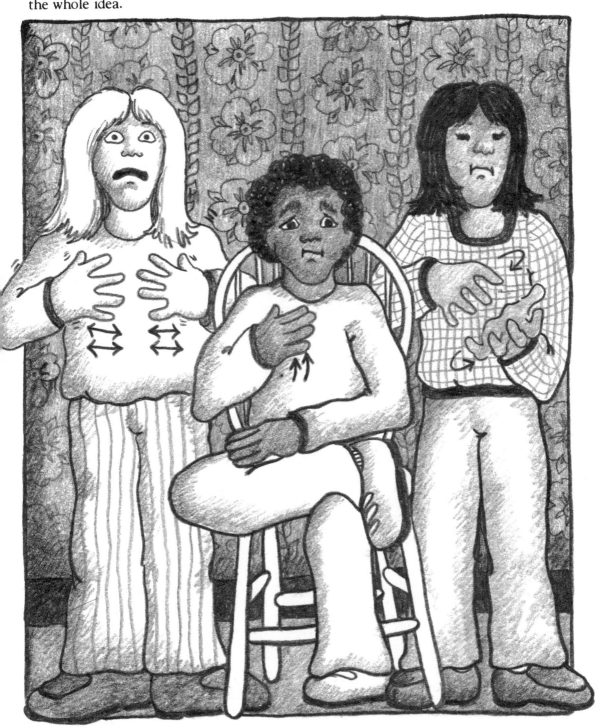

Body language is important, but there's no need to get carried away.

FLEXIBLE FINGERS

Fingers can make great-looking legs.

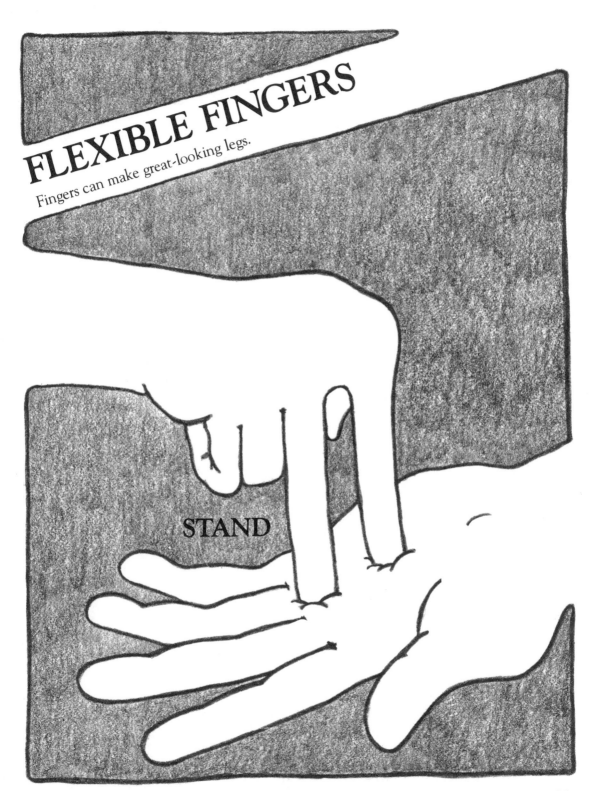

STAND

JUMP

LIE DOWN

KNEEL

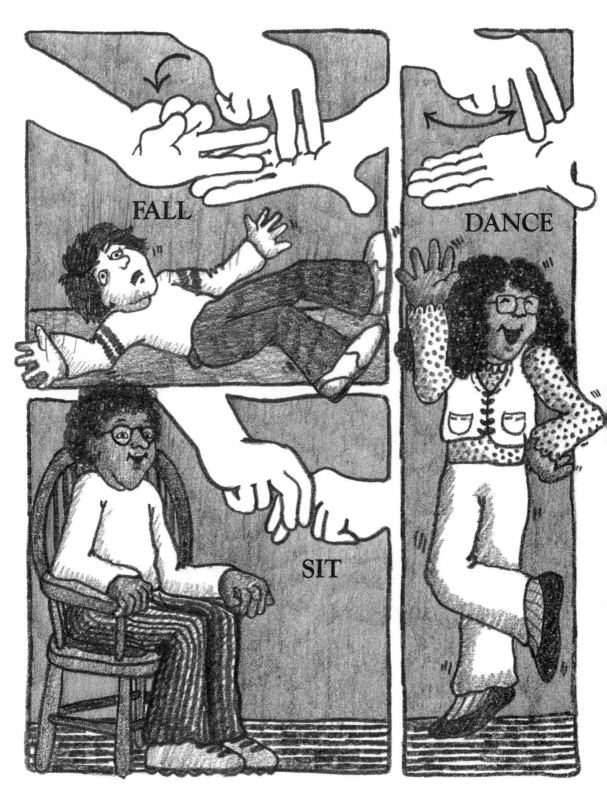

FALL

DANCE

SIT

There's a Spider in Your Milk

CELEBRITY SIGNERS

A few famous friends have dropped by to share their favorite signs.

MONSTER

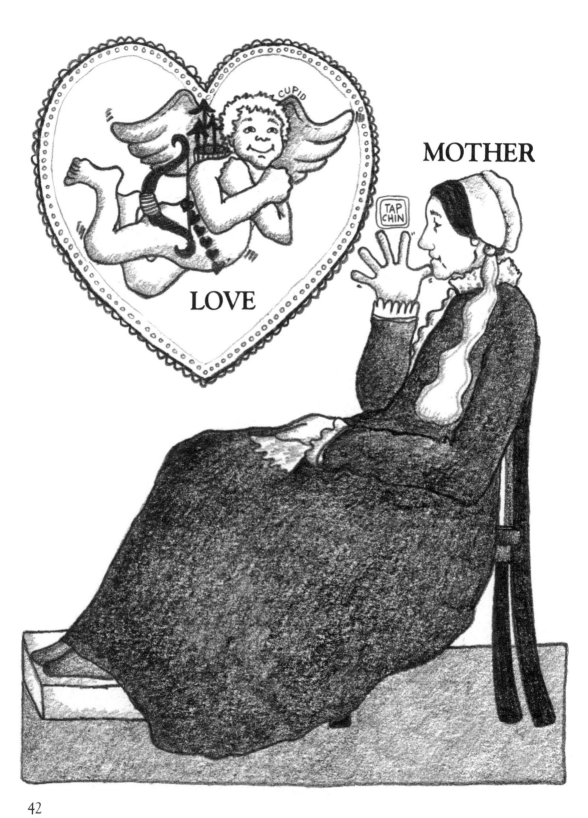

CUPID

LOVE

MOTHER

TAP CHIN

43

SNAKE

MAGIC

STRONG

44

RAIN

NAME

MUSIC

Signs of a Perfect Day

SANDY'S ALARM CLOCK IS JUST ABOUT TO RING. A PERFECT DAY BEGINS IN HER DREAMS...

WAKE UP

PERFECT

DAY

DREAM

DOG

SHE EATS A YUMMY BREAKFAST AND READS THE "SUPER CEREAL COMICS." (SOMETIMES DAD PEEKS.)

SCHOOL IS TERRIFIC TODAY, INCLUDING SANDY'S GRADES! A-, B+, 100, GOLD STAR! 8 WRONG? (OH WELL — CAN'T WIN THEM ALL!)

SPEECH PRACTICE AFTER SCHOOL GOES SO WELL, SANDY LEAVES EARLY FOR TENNIS. SHE PLAYS BETTER THAN EVER!

SANDY AND HER BEST FRIEND, MARIE, ARE STARVING! THEY FINISH A MOUNTAIN OF SPAGHETTI IN NO TIME, AND A HUGE BOWL OF POPCORN "DISAPPEARS" DURING A CAPTIONED T.V. SPECIAL.

NO HOMEWORK! IT'S A MIRACLE! AHHH... TIME FOR A NICE HOT BUBBLE BATH. EVERYTHING IS PERFECT! BUT WAIT A MINUTE. SOMETHING'S WRONG. THE WATER WON'T SHUT OFF! WHAT'S HAPPENING?

FINGERSPELLING

Using 26 hand shapes, you can make all the letters in the alphabet and write them in the air.

WOW!

THE MANUAL ALPHABET

Try using this "airphabet" to fingerspell your name. You'll notice that many of the hand shapes actually look like letters.

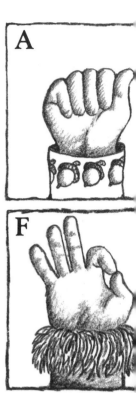

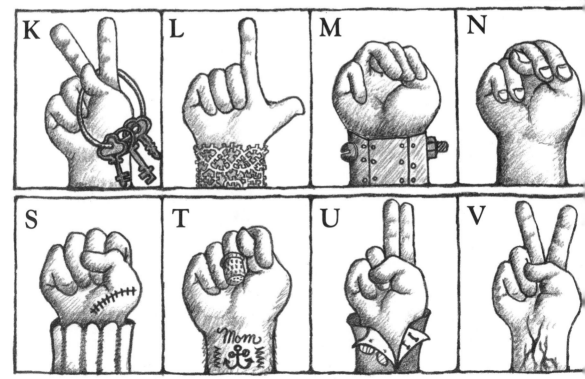

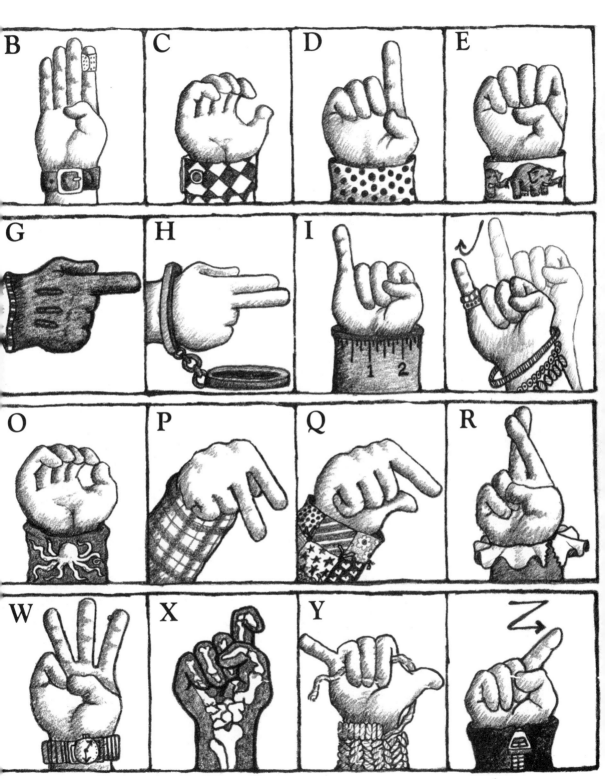

55

People have been fingerspelling for a long time, in fact since about the year 10! Bibles from that time show pages of alphabet hand shapes. Many monks of the middle ages, vowed to silence, used fingerspelling to communicate.

Fingerspelling is so easy, you can even spell
"E-N-C-Y-C-L-O-P-E-D-I-A" with one hand tied behind
your back.
Because signing is faster and more practical, fingerspelling
today is used only for names, places and words that have
no signs.

F IS FOR FRENCH FRIES

F is for French fries. You can make this and other signs by moving the word's first letter in a particular way.

FRENCH FRIES

TAKE A FRENCH FRY WITH AN F

JAM

COP

YELLOW

OWL

WATER

TAP A W ON YOUR CHIN

VISIT

ROTATE 2 V's

LATER

PIVOT AN L FORWARD

61

62

Signing Is a Cinch

HI, SAM!

OH, HI J.B.— GRAB A SEAT!

HEY, SAM — YOU KNOW SANDY, RIGHT? WELL I THINK I FIGURED OUT WHY SHE CAN TALK... IT'S BECAUSE SHE HASN'T ALWAYS BEEN DEAF.

THAT'S NO SECRET, J.B. WHEN DID SHE TELL YOU THAT?

SHE DIDN'T EXACTLY TELL ME. I READ IN A BOOK THAT IT'S MUCH HARDER TO LEARN HOW TO TALK IF YOU'RE BORN DEAF. I FELT KIND OF WEIRD ASKING HER.

HEY, MY MAN, DON'T BE SHY! THERE'S NO FUTURE IN IT! I BET YOU DON'T KNOW THIS, EITHER — I'M THE ONE WHO TAUGHT SANDY SIGN LANGUAGE.

REALLY?

YOU BET!

Why I Learned Sign Language
By
Samuel E. Simmons

My name is Sam. This is the very first picture ever taken of my kid brother, Andy. He was so tiny when he was born that he had to stay at the hospital a few weeks before coming home. I didn't think he was so great. He wasn't much fun—All he did was eat, cry and sleep.

Here's Andy 2 years later trying to get the ball. I liked him better then. At least he could do a few things. He didn't talk and he never looked when I called him, but he was still O.K. at getting the ball. Mom and Dad tried to get him to say stuff, but he only made funny noises. What a kid!

Here's Andy having his first piggy back ride. That was right after the doctor said he was deaf. Mom and Dad were really upset about Andy, but we just kept right on playing.

Here's Andy gulping down his first ball park hot dog. Mom and Dad used to fight a lot then. Mom wanted Andy to learn sign language, but Dad said, "No way!" He wanted Andy to learn how to talk. He said sign language just wouldn't work.

Then one day Dad was watching me and Andy playing and he saw that Andy already used sign language of his own. It took a while, but Dad finally realized that signing was a good way for Andy to talk.

So that's why I learned sign language, in fact, my whole family did. Of course signing was a cinch for me right from the start! Andy goes to speech class now. He's learning how to control his voice to say some words. Last week he said, "Dad," and Dad signed back, "What?" That was a switch!

Andy really is an O.K. kid, but I still feel bad for the poor guy. It must be tough having such a great-looking older brother!

SIGN YOUR NAME

Anyone can have a sign name; just make one up! Most sign names use a person's initial to describe a special habit, personal trait or favorite hobby.

HI. MY NAME IS BOB. I'M KNOWN FOR WEARING MY HAT. IN FACT, I'M NEVER WITHOUT IT. I TAP IT WITH A B TO SIGN MY NAME.

72

Meet Al, Gretchen, Carl and Mary Beth. Who's who?

I'M GRETCHEN, A PAINTER. I PAINT MY PALM BACK AND FORTH WITH A G TO SIGN MY NAME.

MARY BETH HERE. MY SIGN NAME IS MB.

MY NAME IS CARL. MY FAVORITE HOBBY IS MODEL ROCKETRY. MY SIGN NAME IS A C BLASTING OFF.

AL IS SUCH A SHORT NAME. I JUST SPELL IT OUT.

What's the Sign for Scary?

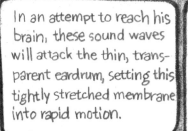

In an attempt to reach his brain, these sound waves will attack the thin, transparent eardrum, setting this tightly stretched membrane into rapid motion.

Will the middle ear be strong enough to receive the attack of such haunting vibrations and pass them along the miniscule trio of bones, deeper still into the dark, murky chambers of the inner ear?

Will there be enough sticky, slimy liquid for these vibes to ooze through the snail-shaped cochlea, forcing the nerve ends to action?

And will these relentless vibrations make it through the final phase of the journey — along the fragile nerve to the brain?

MALLEUS

INCUS

STAPES

OR WILL SOMETHING GO WRONG, LEAVING ME UNABLE TO HEAR AND ENJOY THE HOWLS OF MY VICTIMS? COME SEE THE EARY OUTCOME FOR YOURSELF! WHO KNOWS? YOU MIGHT BE MY "TYPE!"

BLOOD

A CHOOSY WEEK

The sign for sneeze is not surprising, but did you know that people once believed a sneeze meant much more than just a tickle in your nose?

SNEEZE

Sneeze on Monday, sneeze for danger.

Sneeze on Tuesday, kiss a stranger.

Sneeze on Wednesday, sneeze for a letter.

Sneeze on Thursday, get something better.

Sneeze on Friday, sneeze for sorrow.

Sneeze on Saturday, see your sweetheart tomorrow.

Sneeze on Sunday, your safety seek,

Or the devil will take you for the rest of the week.

HOW ARE YOU FEELING?

Whether you're feeling wonderful, curious, hungry or polite, you can be sure there's a sign for you.

WONDERFUL!

I'M FEELING POLITE.

YES

PLEASE

THANK YOU

86

I'M CURIOUS.

WHO?

WHAT?

WHERE?

I'M VERY SAD.

WRING
YOUR
FISTS

HEARTACHE

LONELY

CRY

I'M SO SILLY!

FUNNY   LAUGH   WINK

I'M HUNGRY.

APPLE   POPCORN   HOT DOG

90

I'M FEELING FREE!

KIDS SUMMER VACATION

Say It in Sign Language

SIGNING OFF

The best way to improve your signing is by practicing with people who use sign language all the time. When you do this, you will surely find that there is more than one way to sign certain ideas. You may also discover that some signs change over time or vary slightly from place to place.

There are more than 150 signs in A SHOW OF HANDS, but this is only a beginning. So, say it in sign language whenever you can and "watch" your vocabulary grow.

THE SIGNS